PRAISE FOR

Become an Ideal Head of School Candidate

Wow! With great wisdom, Lydia Musher has successfully brought clarity to an often complex and murky process that is sure to help Head of School candidates for years to come. The insights into the 'unwritten' elements of what search committees are looking for make me wish that I had this resource at the start of my career.

— RABBI AVERY JOEL,
Head of School, Fuchs Mizrachi School, Beachwood, Ohio

The independent school world and its many leaders are very fortunate to have a remarkable resource of this kind.

—PAUL ASTIN,
Head of School, Manzanita School, Topanga, California

"It is not often one finds a resource that is relevant, engaging, and easy to follow. As an administrator and educator, we never have enough hours in the day, so having a book organized and written like Become an Ideal Head of School Candidate is very much welcomed and needed!"

—JENNIFER LeVINE,
Head of School, Beth Yeshurun Day School, Houston, Texas

What an amazing guide to becoming a great candidate for the Head of School role. Lydia Musher breaks the search process down into digestible pieces and easy-to-remember acronyms so you will be prepared every step of the way. I wish I had a resource like this years ago!

—Dr. Paul Oberman,
Head of School, Beren Academy, Houston, Texas

The laser-sharp focus of this book on preparing for and navigating the journey to become a head of school make it a uniquely valuable resource for advancing professional careers in educational leadership.

—Cedar Oliver,
Director of School, Waldorf School of Mass. Bay, Belmont, Massachusetts

You have done a great job of dissecting the key elements needed to provide a candidate with the advice they need to be successful. Easy to read and with lots of input from existing heads that gives the whole material credibility.

—Nathan Washer,
Head of School, Wichita Collegiate School, Wichita, Kansas

[A] fascinating book - wish it had been available some years ago when I began this journey.

—TOM WILSCHUTZ,
Head of School, Solebury School, New Hope, Pennsylvania

A helpful and eminently usable guide for those aspiring to headship.

—DAVE MULLEN,
Interim Head of School, Wye River Upper School, Centreville, Maryland

BECOME AN IDEAL
HEAD OF SCHOOL
CANDIDATE

LYDIA MUSHER

AUTHOR, HIRE AN IDEAL HEAD OF SHCOOL
PRESIDENT, TRADITION SEARCH PARTNERS

Become an Ideal Head of School Candidate
(cc) 2021 Lydia Musher
President, Tradition Search Partners
Author, Hire an Ideal Head of School

ISBN 978-1-7359878-4-2 (Paperback)
ISBN 978-1-7359878-3-5 (eBook)
ISBN 978-1-7359878-5-9 (Audiobook)
Library of Congress Control Number: 2021907416

Published by Lydia Musher, Tradition Search Partners, Houston, Texas, USA

First paperback edition April 2021
First eBook edition April 2021
First audiobook edition July 2021

THIS BOOK IS DEDICATED TO MY CHILDREN

Talia, my favorite
Avi, my favorite
Noah, my favorite
and Eli, my favorite

TABLE OF CONTENTS

a. About You

This book will help you prepare to obtain an ideal Head of School role, whether you are applying now or years down the road.

I wrote this book for you if you intend to apply for Headships soon from your position as an Associate Head, Assistant Head, Division Head, Admissions Director, Advancement Director, or as a school outsider with relevant experience.

This book will also work well for you if you are currently a Head of School, Interim Head of School, or Acting Head of School preparing to apply for your next role in a larger school. Or maybe you're interested in finding a school that better serves your educational philosophy, geographic preferences, or career goals.

This book offers ideal long-term preparation for you if you're a young teacher, an experienced teacher-leader, a department chair, or other educator considering your long-term plans.

Finally, this book will also help you if you're a school board member or search-committee member interested in learning about the search process from a candidate's perspective. What advice do candidates get, and what do experienced Heads say about the process from their perspectives?

In many ways, the Head of School recruitment process is uniquely time-consuming, risky, and emotional for independent schools. The process can be opaque or downright confusing to candidates — and challenging for school trustees, too.

To help you succeed at this complex process, this short book contains insights about processes, techniques to utilize, and case studies from scores of Heads of School. My experience as a founder and president of a boutique Head of School search firm that has handled countless searches ties these data together.

You can read this book in two to three hours. That way, you can read this book while running a school or division, maintaining a personal life, and finishing whatever continuing education you're pursuing. In order to keep it short, we offer a lot of helpful additional resources, including an interactive workbook, at http://TraditionSearchPartners.com/Become for you to download and use as needed without cluttering up the pages here.

I hope you find this book useful as you work through the process of finding your first or next Headship. If you have any questions, please email us at become@TraditionSearchPartners.com. I reply to my emails individually and would be delighted to help you.

b. About the Author

I am the president and co-founder of the boutique executive-search firm Tradition Search Partners. Tradition serves the boards of independent schools seeking to make a leadership change through executive recruitment and strategic advising.

Additionally, I taught for seven years in the top-twenty business school at Rice University. I have served in many leadership roles in the technology and nonprofit sectors during my more than twenty-year career.

I hold an M.B.A. from The Wharton School of the University of Pennsylvania, focused on marketing and entrepreneurship as well as M.Eng. and Sc.B. degrees in computer science from the Massachusetts Institute of Technology.

This book is my second in the field based on my experience placing Heads of School at independent schools. My first, *Hire an Ideal Head of School (With or Without a Search Firm)*, lays out the entire process from the perspective of a school board member or search-committee member. If you'd like to understand the process from a school's perspective, I'd encourage you to check it out at http://TraditionSearchPartners.com/Ideal or buy the book at your favorite bookseller.

In addition to my experience, I include quotes and data from close to 100 Heads of School who generously contributed to this book. Many agreed to be interviewed over video, while others submitted written thoughts via survey or email. Unless otherwise stated, a quote from a Head of School comes from an interview they granted to me directly and permitted me to use in this book. I am immensely indebted to all of them and name them individually where permitted to do so.

If you'd like to learn more about us or contact us, please visit http://TraditionSearchPartners.com/Become. This website is a great place to find resources to download as you undertake your search.

c. What this Book Covers & Doesn't Cover

This book covers the process of getting the Head of School job that you want by becoming the "ideal" Head of School candidate. Importantly, this book is not about how to *be* a great Head of School, just how to *get* the job.

There should be huge overlaps between getting the job and doing the job because the selection process *should* cause you to demonstrate your ability to *do* the job. For this reason, many of the Heads of School talked more about doing the job than getting the job.

If you're looking for a book on *being* an ideal Head of School (as opposed to an ideal *candidate*), I recommend the long and comprehensive *The Head's Handbook,* printed by the National Association of Independent Schools (NAIS). In the book, authors Jay Riven and Gene Batiste answer questions such as:

- What advice can Heads give you that will make the job easier?

- How can Heads cope with and master the many roles of Headships these days?

- How does the Head's family relate effectively to the campus community?

- How do Heads successfully deal with crises?

- How do they best cultivate relationships with the community?

- How might Headships change in the future?

But *until* you land that job, you've found the right book right here.

d. How this Book Works

Like my first book, *Hire an Ideal Head of School: With or Without a Search Firm*, this book will get you up to speed quickly and easily.

Chapter 1. The Written Requirements breaks down the written job descriptions and advertisements you will encounter as you proceed through your search. We'll talk about how to build up the necessary "CREST" skill sets like people management, financial stewardship, and board management. We'll also discuss how search committees will evaluate these skills, and how to market yourself effectively in each of these areas.

In Chapter 2. The Unwritten Requirements, we'll talk about the unspoken ways in which boards, administrators, faculty, and parents will evaluate you. Those unspoken rules are even more important than the overtly stated job requirements. From testing your stamina and energy levels during fourteen-hour-long days of finalist visits to engaging your spouse in a way that helps you both, we'll cover everything unspoken about the process.

Chapter 3. How the Process Typically Works will walk you through the entire process, from finding roles and submitting your resume, to phone screenings, on-site finalist visits, and salary negotiation. This chapter is obviously immediately helpful if you're about to embark on a search or are already involved in a search. It also provides great information for building your resume earlier in your career.

Chapter 4. Paths presents case studies that represent different ways to become a Head. These case studies introduce you to current Heads of School and their different paths to the role. Some are traditional, and others are non-traditional: admissions directors who became heads, people who started their own schools, and more. I hope this chapter will help you see yourself on one or more of the pathways to become a Head of School and help you learn some tricks of each trade.

Finally, the Conclusions chapter helps you decide what to do next, depending on how long you have: whether you're neck-deep in a search and want to refine your outcome, if you're a year away from starting the process, or if you're looking years ahead to prepare yourself effectively. The accompanying workbook I've created at http://TraditionSearchPartners.com/Become will help you use your conclusions to your advantage, as well.

A word about terminology: throughout this book, I tend to use the word "independent" to refer to tuition-charging secular and parochial schools interchangeably.

Let's get started.

CHAPTER ONE

The Written Requirements

When I see a successful Head, I know that there is alignment between the Head and the School, not just in terms of educational philosophy, but also in what the school needs at a given time. It is interesting to me that what my school needs now is entirely different than what we needed seven years ago when I was hired. This is not to say that I am not aligned now, but seven years ago, my strengths aligned with the greatest needs of the school at the time and that made all the difference.

—JASON LOPEZ,
The Pegasus School, Huntington Beach, CA

When I started interviewing Heads of School for this book, I was surprised to hear how much they focused on "finding the right school," "finding the right fit," or "finding the right alignment between school and Head." This principle makes sense, of course: find a school that needs your strengths and can make accommodations for your weaknesses. Find a school where you can shine. We'll dig into this good advice in more detail in Chapter 2. The Unwritten Requirements.

But before starting the process (or after finding the perfect potential school), every candidate would benefit from knowing the truth: there are some characteristics, skills, and experiences that virtually every school board and search committee wants. I created the CREST Framework to describe the five tools that every school wants in a Head:

- C: Communication Skills
- R: Responsibility for People
- E: Enrollment Management
- S: Stewardship of Finances
- T: Technical Expertise as a Master Educator

We cover these tools in this chapter because they are common to almost all searches and are a valuable place to start. However:

> *The SIZE of the school is fundamental to what the job entails. At a small school, with little additional administration, the Head may do everything from teach and coach to student discipline and even light facility repairs. At a large school, contact with the kids is limited, you are in meetings all day, and most of the work is 'institutional visioning.' You are wise if you know what kind of job you really want and seek a school that fits what you are good at.*

> —GARY TAYLOR,

> *Head of School, Trinity Episcopal School, New Orleans, Louisiana*

Each school will *rank* these five tools differently based on the current state of the school. When search committees write their job advertisements and opportunity statements, they consider their priorities in hiring. For example, some schools will need a very strong educational leader but deprioritize financial management. First (for better or worse), boards and search committees tend to prioritize skills that the outgoing or previous head lacked. Secondly, they tend to deprioritize skills that other people on campus have, so if their senior-admin team has a Chief Financial Officer, they won't be looking for a head with super-strong financial chops. Third, schools are usually looking to solve particular problems, often that of increasing enrollment in a mission-aligned and financially sustainable way. You can read a lot of these aims and preferences in the job advertisement, particularly if you read between the lines a bit.

C: Communication Skills

[D]on't underestimate the power of laughter. In my finalist interview, they had me meet with the entire staff (180 people) in the auditorium and I started the hour with a story that made them all laugh a lot. Two years later there are staff who still bring it up. Apparently the other two finalists were very serious in their time in front of the staff. It wasn't just about that of course, but I do think it made a difference.

—NATHAN WASHER,
Head of School, Wichita Collegiate, Wichita, Kansas

Officially, "communication skills" refers to three tools: writing; one-on-one interpersonal communication with adults or students; and public speaking to audiences of adults, students, or a mixed-aged audience. In a real sense, communication skills are the most important skills any leader possesses. You'll find some version of this requirement in nearly every job description, and it is an important element in all of them: interacting with people is the exhausting central work of a Head of School.

The interview process aptly tests the oral communication skills of aspiring Heads of School. You'll participate in a large number of one-on-one interviews by phone, on video, and in person. You'll be interviewed by large groups of people, possibly facing "fastball questions" from "25 board members and their spouses," as The Fletcher School's Head of School Brent Betit described in his interview process for one Headship. Often, committees will also ask you to prepare a slide presentation answering a specific prompt from "Why do you want to be our Head of School?" to "Describe your educational philosophy."

During group meetings, it is incredibly important to organize your thoughts and to reply to questions quickly and clearly. One board president, Tom Henschel of Children's Community School in Los Angeles, said that clarity of thought made a difference in choosing among well-qualified candidates. One candidate was "pleasant to listen to but didn't move the conversation forward. It took him two paragraphs to get to the gist of his response." Even if the response was ultimately a strong one, the candidate had lost the momentum of the conversation by the time he got to his point. Don't make the same mistake in your responses.

Henschel further offers, "[The best candidates] had real clarity about who they were. They were showing up with their brand and their flavor distinct. It made some challenging choices, but it made it really helpful for us."

In terms of interpersonal skills, learn to make pleasant small talk. Pay attention when people talk; put down your phone. Make sure to greet and speak with everyone you meet at a school, from the receptionist to the maintenance staff to the large donors and the executive board. If you are allowed to meet children, meet them at their level both physically and emotionally. Smile on campus like you're really happy to be there. Avoid asking any questions that might make people feel criticized during the interview process. Send grammatically correct thank-you notes to people who meet with you.

Strengthening this skill set:

- Writing: If you aren't currently the person responsible for writing your school's regular newsletter, ask if you can get involved in doing so. Find out what your readers want and the format they find easiest to read. Consider utilizing tools like Grammarly that help you ensure you are producing quality written communication for all of your writing.

- Interpersonal skills: Develop an interest in and respect for the experiences of others. Learn to ask questions and listen without interrupting. Chapter 2. The Unwritten Requirements will present more on interpersonal skills.

- Public speaking: Seek opportunities to speak in public on behalf of your school or other community organizations. If you really fear public speaking, join Toastmasters or take a local continuing-education course to improve your confidence.

- Seek feedback: Ask people you trust about which of your communication skills is a strength and which is a weakness.

R: Responsibility for People

Candidates tend to think it is financial management that features heavily in the roster of skills that search committees are looking for. Some basic familiarity with budgets and strategic financial planning, as well as fundraising, are undoubtedly important. But, in this era, it is people management and brand management that figure most heavily. How well can you motivate, inspire, and organize people to work towards a shared vision of your school that aligns with the strategic direction of the school.

—Dr. Rodney Glasgow,
Head of School, Sandy Spring Friends School, Sandy Spring, Maryland

After communication skills, supervision of people is the most consistently sought-after skill for a Head of School. Ideally, you'd have five or more years as a Head of School, Associate Head,

Assistant Head, or at least Division Head to gain supervisory experience.

In addition, you'd ideally have five years of experience with the peculiar, double-edged sword of interacting with a board of trustees or a board of directors. Yes, technically, the board hires, fires, and evaluates the Head. However, as the Head, you also help select your bosses, own your relationships with them, and ensure that they get the information they need to make the best possible governance choices. Familiarity with the board isn't just about knowing Robert's Rules of Order and how to change inappropriate by-laws; it's about knowing your power and using it effectively. When a Head tells me they had a bad relationship with the board, I believe them, but I also think they likely did not handle their part of that essential relationship-building task effectively.

The best preparation for the application process is to build your experience with people management slowly over a period of years. There is simply no substitute, no course, no doctoral program that substitutes for experience with managing people, helping them to be successful in their work in service of a shared vision.

Michael Robinson, Head of School at Stuart Hall in Staunton, Virginia, built his leadership experience slowly. He volunteered for committee work to show his ability to lead a group even before he officially managed anyone. He was transparent with his Head of School that he was interested in becoming a Head of School someday while he simultaneously assured the sitting Head that he wasn't immediately out for his job. Michael, a veteran sports coach, asked for feedback often, "practice, performance, execution, reflection" was his mantra.

If you're a Head now, take active responsibility for your one-on-one relationship with each board member. Learn to introduce your ideas one-on-one in private and provide meaningful information in public. Don't be surprised by a coup d'etat for which you weren't prepared. And don't fall into the all-too-easy trap of blaming your board members for a breakdown in that relationship the next time you interview for a new position.

If you're an Associate or Assistant Head, see if your Head will let you present regularly at board meetings, contribute to the preparation of her reports, and meet with senior board members to establish strong relationships on her behalf. Ask your Head if you can serve on a board sub-committee like budget, finance, investment, or advancement if such committees exist. These direct interactions will help build your board-management skills.

If you're just getting started in your career, be smart: never run to the board with your day-to-day concerns. It's a rookie mistake for young teachers to think that complaining to a trustee will solve an interpersonal conflict with the Head of School. Early career is not the time to burn bridges; it's the time for you to volunteer for committee work and establish yourself as an up-and-coming manager.

E: Enrollment Management

He who has a thing to sell / and goes and whispers in a well / is not so apt to get the dollars / as he who climbs a tree and hollers!

—AUTHOR UNKNOWN

From my perspective, there are two fundamental states in which an independent school can find itself: having a waitlist or not having a waitlist. The school's state will influence its committee's level of attention to your experience with enrollment management: marketing, recruitment, retention, and community building.

For schools with waitlists, marketing the school is likely *not* their central problem. They have a product that people want to buy (whether with tuition in an independent school or with their application in a charter school). Prospective parents are aware of the school's value, and they want it. Schools with waitlists are the happy ones, and they're not going to be looking for their next Head of School to work marketing miracles.

Schools without waitlists are the ones looking for miracle workers to grow their enrollment overnight without offering massive financial incentives and without changing their admissions standards. For schools with empty desks (that is, space for more students), a track record of success with increasing enrollment in a financially sustainable and mission-aligned way will be of primary importance.

One Head of School told me that "schools think they will get a magic leader who will solve all of their [enrollment] problems." Yet "magic" is hard to explain, describe, implement, teach, or reproduce. Some ideas for learning to "climb the tree and holler" for your school:

- Be known personally for your relentless positivity and support for the school. If you're upset about something that happened, talk with your parents or partner about it, not your students' parents, students, or colleagues. Schools are not looking for leaders who vent their negativity "authentically."

- Join local networking groups, online and offline. Social media is helpful, but so are old-fashioned clubs like the Rotary Club or its equivalent. Find out what's prevalent in your area. Whenever possible, represent your school professionally, positively, and proactively.

- If your school doesn't have an alumni group, ask if you can help build one. Alumni often send their children to the school or donate money. You can crowdsource an alumni database for free with the help of five to ten alumni and their connections. If your school already has an Alumni program, ask to get involved.

- If your school doesn't have a parent ambassador program, ask if you can help build one. If it does exist, ask to get involved. Parent ambassador programs help with retention and recruitment. As appropriate, you may want to ask to host parlor meetings at your house or facilitate a meeting at the house of a popular parent.

- Your school likely has a parent-teacher organization (PTO), parent-teacher association (PTA), or parent guild. Ask if you can be a liaison to this program to build your retention programs and ensure high-quality relationships between parents and the school.

- Take a simple marketing course on Coursera or some other online platform to learn marketing vocabulary.

- Sign up for a Google Alert (http://google.com/alerts) to be notified by email any time your school's name shows up online. Knowing what people are saying on the Internet about your school is incredibly valuable. (While you're at it, add an alert for your name, too.)

- Highlight these experiences in your interviews with schools without waitlists.

S: Stewardship of Finances

There can be significant differences in [job requirements] depending on the school. As a generalization, small and large schools might value different skills. A large school will have someone in charge of each bucket - admissions, finances, faculty, etc. - while a small school might require more hands-on leadership in these areas.

—DOUGLAS NORRY,
Head of School, Triangle Day School, Durham, North Carolina

All schools need Heads with the three financial-stewardship skills: budgeting, finance, and fundraising. The extent of that need (and most needs) depends a lot on the school's size. You'll hear that dependency a lot in this book. (The only skill that isn't more or less important based on school size is communication, as discussed above; every school needs a Head with solid communication skills.)

At a large school, a Head will likely have a Chief Financial Officer (CFO) for finance and budgeting, a business manager and a business office for additional budget-related matters, and a large, professional Advancement team for fundraising. Your role will be to direct and oversee these teams to achieve strategic goals like building a new building or creating a new high school.

At a tiny school, you will have few to none of these people. You will probably create the budget yourself with the help of the board treasurer and a bookkeeper. You will do the fundraising, again, maybe with the assistance of a part-time helper or parent volunteer. If you have major financial issues like managing an endowment, paying off loans, or recovering from a devastating flood in Texas or fire in California, you may similarly rely on volunteer and part-time help. A lot of the work and a lot of the responsibility will fall on your shoulders.

One Head who asked to remain anonymous for this book said that boards want to know, "Do you have budget experience, development, fundraising experience, and enrollment, particularly if you have a school that is small and doesn't have large offices for them, CFO, Director of Development, and Director of Admissions? That has been a big learning curve for me." This Head is not alone: financial stewardship is the part of the job most unlike other jobs that most Heads hold before their first Headship, so it's the steepest learning curve for almost all incoming Heads.

It's hard to evaluate candidates for financial competence during the interview process, so "boards are interested in scale," says Nancy Leaderman, Head of School at The Shalom School of Sacramento, California. Schools with a $50 million budget typically look at a candidate's track record in terms of the size of the budgets they have managed previously. They're likely interested in Heads who have previously managed budgets in their range. If they interview a candidate who's been a Head at a school with a two-million-dollar budget, they're likely to worry about the jump up from two to fifty million dollars.

The same is true for fundraising: If the most you've raised is $10,000 for a new piece of playground equipment, there will be some concern from school boards about whether you can raise $10M for their capital campaign for a new football stadium.

On the other hand, fundraising is not that complicated. Nicole du Fauchard, Head of School at The Advent School in Boston, Massachusetts, states, "If you can balance your checkbook at home, $1 there translates into $1M in a school budget. Fundraising is the same: five dollars is five million dollars. I think [kindergarten] teachers are the best fundraisers [because of how they connect with donors about what they do]."

Heads themselves disagree on how important this part of the job itself is. Some Heads, like Col. David Coggins of Fork Union Military Academy in Fork Union, Virginia, think it is the most important part of the job:

"Private schools, for-profit or not, are businesses and should be led by successful business leaders who have a passion for the school's mission — not coaches, preachers or teachers with little/no experience in raising, saving money, balancing a budget, marketing, [human resources], or campus master plans [and] infrastructure."

Others disagree. Drew Casertano has served as the Head of School at Millbrook School in Millbrook, NY, for more than 30 years. We'll talk with him more in Chapter 4, Section b. The Internal Candidate, to hear how he grooms his successor. Drew worries about hiring committees' being "enamored with the finance side, the corporate" part of running a school.

You are well prepared in the Financial Stewardship arena to apply for a school's Head position if you have raised money approximately in proportion to the school's total fundraising and if you have managed a budget in proportion to the size of that school's budget.

It can be hard to build this track record, but it's not impossible. If you do not yet have this track record, proactively create it. First, ask if you can volunteer to participate in fundraising efforts and budget-related matters for your school. If your Head of School is territorial, you might ask if you can watch and learn from her experience. If your Head of School is interested in coaching and mentoring you, you might ask if you can help more directly. If neither of these is possible, seek out the opportunity to run a program like a summer camp where you'd own an entire budget. This experience may be small, but it's definitely better than nothing.

T: Technical Expertise as a Master Educator

It has been my experience that Heads of Schools who have teaching experience are more credible in the eyes of the teachers they serve.

—CARRIE KRIES,
Head of School, Gladwyne Montessori,
Gladwyne, Pennsylvania

In a Head of School search, "technical expertise" refers to the extent to which you as a candidate are a master educator in your own right: years of classroom experience at the highest grade levels offered by the school at which you want a job, advanced degrees in education or administration, and professional network. Here again, the importance of technical mastery in the hiring process depends greatly on the school's size.

A large school is likely to have strong principals in each division. Strong principals don't need strong educators to tell them how to run their divisions. They need Heads with the skills described above: strong communicators, financial stewardship, people management, and enrollment management.

Pro tip: If you find yourself involved in a search for a large school (over 300 students, say) where you're asked lots of technical questions about your abilities as an educator, you can feel relatively confident that they need a leadership overhaul at the principal level. You'll meet with the principals in the hiring process and can do a bit of an assessment of them based on the sophistication of the questions they ask you.

Small schools are usually looking for expert educators. You may be the *only* administrator at the very smallest schools, in which case you're responsible for everything from classroom supervision to curriculum selection to scope and sequence. In a school with a principal or two, a Head is often still tasked with ensuring the programs' quality.

If you are able to apply for one of the nationally recognized training programs for aspiring and new Heads, these programs are an excellent step in the process. In order to keep an up-to-date list of these programs, I have linked them from http://TraditionSearchPartners. com/Become for your use. There are also doctoral programs in education leadership; some focus on particular types of schools, which can help build administrators' resumes very effectively.

Additionally, schools tend to look for leaders with significant experience at the highest educational level they offer. For example, a nursery and primary school that starts at fifteen months and goes through fifth grade will want someone who's taught at the upper-elementary level and managed an elementary school before. Similarly, a school that takes students starting in kindergarten and graduates them after twelfth grade will want someone with significant high-school experience. Do what you can to develop experience, education, and credentialing at the highest level you want to manage.

Finally, some very concrete advice about building a reputation for technical expertise in educational leadership:

> *I encourage [aspiring Heads of School] to go on accreditation visits [of other schools as part of their own accrediting organization] and publish articles in educational journals.*
>
> —DR. PAUL OBERMAN,
> *Beren Academy, Houston, Texas*

What if you don't have much classroom experience, your degrees aren't in education or educational administration, and your professional network isn't in educational leadership? Nicole du Fauchard, the Advent School Head we met above, advocates for making explicit connections between your experience and the role's technical needs. For example, you may have worked as an adjunct instructor at a local college, requiring you to do many of the same tasks as a secondary school teacher. You may have developed a strong reputation as a leader in your professional networks and can transfer that skill set to developing a strong professional network in education administration.

Other Heads agree:

> *Before becoming a head of school, I worked in secondary school placement at one school in NYC and in admissions at another NYC school. Learning about enrollment from*

both sides of the desk, so to speak, was valuable experi-
ence. I learned a lot about financial leadership by serv-
ing on the board of an educational non-profit. Serving
on a board taught me a lot about people, governance,
non-profit finance, and fundraising.

—JOY HURD,
Head of School at Lake Forest Country
Day School in Lake Forest, Illinois,

If you are looking for a Head of School position right now, it's never too late to get involved in regional and national professional networks and take committee-leadership positions if you haven't already.

If you are years away from your future search, now is *definitely* the time to get involved at this level. These networks help build your reputation as a leader in your field; they will also facilitate mutually beneficial relationships: mentorship, referrals, and more.

CHAPTER TWO

The Unwritten Requirements

We covered the CREST Framework for written job requirements in Chapter 1. The Written Requirements ("CREST"). However, if you were to look only at the written requirements for a position or read only the previous chapter, you would be wholly unprepared for the complexities of the Head of School search process.

The trick is that most jobs in most industries have profoundly complex and important unwritten requirements, and the Head of School position has more than most. Several school leaders told me some version of this summary: "They're paying you to stay calm when no one else is." This section will break down what it means for a Head to be "the grownup in the room" in more detail and offer suggestions for demonstrating this skill during the hiring process.

In part a. The FACTS Framework: Unwritten Requirements, we'll talk about the five major, unwritten requirements of the Head of School job and how to master and demonstrate them.

- F: Fit
- A: Activity level
- C: Connection
- T: Trust
- S: SELF Management

In part b. The SELF Management Framework, we will delve more deeply into the "S" above: what it means to manage oneself from the perspective of the Head of School search process:

- S: Surroundings
- E: Events
- L: Look
- F: Feelings

Finally, in part c. The Really Hard Parts: Partners and Prejudice, we will talk about the difficult, negative ways in which prejudice enters the hiring scene.

a. The FACTS Framework: The Unwritten Requirements

In this section, we are going to talk about the ways that search committees will evaluate you that you won't find written in any job description:

F: Fit

> *Culture is everything, and it is the hardest thing to com-municate and elicit, for both parties, and for search committees to quantify and predict in the hiring pro-cess. Connection [to the community] is so closely related to Culture...New Heads who have the skills needed to quickly build rapport can afford themselves the time*

and opportunity to learn culture. But Culture is ev-erything...

—PAUL ZANOWSKI,
Head of School, Woodlawn School, Mooresville, North Carolina

Hiring a Head of School is a moment of *tremendous* risk for a school. If a school hires the wrong Head, the school could experience excessive faculty turnover, a decline in enrollment, sustain painful financial damage, or even — in extreme cases — close the school. Therefore, the simple fact is that the less of a risk you present to an employer, the more likely they will hire you. Your job as a candidate is to make it clear that you are simultaneously a low-risk candidate and still a strong and exciting candidate. It's a hard balancing act, especially for a candidate to navigate with integrity.

One of the most effective ways you can present yourself as a low-risk candidate is by highlighting your similarity with the community, utilizing the cognitive bias known as "in-grouping." According to the American Psychology Association[1], the "in-group bias" is "the tendency to favor one's own group, its members, its characteristics, and its products, particularly in reference to other groups. The favoring of the in-group tends to be more pronounced than the rejection of the outgroup, but both tendencies become more pronounced during periods of intergroup contact. At the regional, cultural, or national level, this bias is often termed ethnocentrism."

---

[1]   https://dictionary.apa.org/ingroup-bias

Appearing to be part of the school's group will help the school feel that you are "one of them" and that hiring you is less risky and more comfortable. There are many ways to demonstrate in-grouping, again provided that you do so earnestly and with integrity. It would be a net loss to present yourself as something that you aren't because it would lead to your immediate failure as a Head of that school.

- Mission: You have a personal connection to the mission of the school. Perhaps you were a boarding-school student yourself and are being considered for the role of Head of a boarding school. Perhaps you are the father of a child with autism, and you are applying for a Headship of a school for children with autism. Perhaps the school is Episcopal, and you attend an Episcopal church. The Head of School is the school's flag bearer, so a personal connection to the school's mission is essential.

- Connection with the community: You grew up in the community, went to the school yourself, taught at the school before, lived in the geographic area or even a similar area, you know parents or faculty members in the community.

- Educational philosophy: If the school where you're interviewing is a Montessori school and you have dedicated your life to the Waldorf or Charlotte Mason teaching philosophies, expect questions. On the other hand, if the school is a school well-aligned with your experience, they will expect you to ooze excitement about your shared philosophy.

- Culture fit: It helps if you are "one of them." You dress like they do, you talk like they do, you have similar hobbies, your family structure is similar to that of the average parent. Don't fake any of these things, but know that earnestly "mirroring" does help.

- Preparation: As we will discuss at various times throughout this book, be prepared for each interview. I recommend keeping a section in a binder about each school in which you're interested.

- Demonstrated interest: Finally, it helps to appear interested. At some point late in the process, it is highly likely that the committee chair or board chair will ask you, "If offered the position, will you accept it?" If the answer is "Absolutely," it is worth offering this information as early as appropriate. Saying to the recruiter, "If offered the position, I'd be excited to accept it," can help to tip the scales in your favor. So can genuine expressions of interest and enthusiasm throughout the process.

Several years ago, I facilitated a search for a large, East coast independent school. The school was widely regarded as an excellent school both academically and holistically, and it was filled to capacity with a waiting list at several grade levels. One of the finalist candidates was a committed "progressive" Head of School looking for a "progressive" school for her next Headship. It's important to know yourself and what you're looking for in a school. She used the word "progressive" in every conversation, interview, and email. Because the school I represented was not a self-identified "progressive" school, they were put off by her strongly stated philosophical identity. It worked well: she ended up at a school that was a much better fit for her, and the school hired a Head that was a much better fit for its educational philosophy.

A: Activity Level

In non-pandemic times, a normal interview day might start at 8 am and end at 10 pm without a break. There are group meetings with parents, group meetings with faculty members, individual meetings with senior administrators, a walking tour of the campus, an analysis of documents, receptions with your partner, a prepared presentation before the board, and a meeting with the search committee.

All in all, the Head of School interview process is almost comically exhausting. Most Heads of School I interviewed seem to think that the exhausting nature of the process is by design, to see how you function under pressure.

In the United States, the search committee will all expect you to smile all day long unless you're discussing a serious matter like an injury to a child or a death in the community. They want to see you make eye contact, as eye contact is considered by many to be a mark of honesty and self-confidence. Parents, board members, and donors especially want to see charisma, defined by author Olivia Fox Cabane in the book *The Charisma Myth* as "warmth, power, and presence." Faculty members want you to be curious and attentive and express real opinions, mostly about how actively you will listen to them. (I'm mostly joking here.) The process of hiring Heads of School decidedly favors extroverts in many ways, including this one.

We will talk a little more about stamina in Chapter 3. How the Process Typically Works, in part f. In-Person Interviews.

C: Collaborative Leadership

> *In order to go fast, you must first go slow — aim to build relationships, make connections, understand the history and the current state of the organization first before trying to implement new ideas. You have to work hard to get people on board and build trust in the leadership before making headway down the fast lane!*
>
> —INTERIM HEAD OF SCHOOL RACHEL SECHLER,
> *Ashbrook Independent School, Corvallis, Oregon*

Most schools looking for a new Head are also aiming for other changes in the school itself. Of course, some very successful Heads retire after twenty years leaving behind a well-running school with a well-prepared successor, but these cases are unusual (and rarely result in a search in any event).

When you're being considered as a future Head of School, you have a thin line to walk. You have to be an experienced and expert educational leader while also demonstrating that you're trying to learn about the school. You're not just walking in to make sweeping, frightening changes that make people nervous with inadequate information.

If you get to the group-meeting part of the hiring process, I promise you that there will be someone in the room (often a board member) who will be offended if you express a specific vision for their school without first being at the school for a year. The problem is that there will be a second person (often a faculty member) who will be put off if you don't have a specific vision for the school (based on your extensive research about the school and your vast experience and education). I've been in this meeting many times as a facilitator. This balancing act is one of the most challenging to manage in the entire interview process.

The magic message is something along the lines of, "Here's how I've done it before and/or here's what I know, here's the collaborative element I'd need to build with your school."

Perhaps you need to bring a committee together to understand the history of the enrollment problem, to introduce you to the influential parents in the community, and to understand the school's strengths and weaknesses in its competitive marketplace. These are the things you'd articulate in the third part of the magic message. Here's what I know, and here's what I would need to learn. In so doing, you communicate knowledge *and* wisdom, vision *and* collaboration.

T: Trust

> *There are foundational traits... that I believe are critical: INTEGRITY, INTELLIGENCE, ENERGY. If these are missing, none of the [other skills] will make much difference.*
>
> —DIANE BORGMANN,
> *Head of School, Sycamore School, Indianapolis, Indiana*

In a search that my firm facilitated recently, a particularly strong candidate visited with different groups of stakeholders, as usual. One search-committee member attended two different meetings with the candidate (which is also pretty normal as search-committee members are almost always also parents, board members, or faculty). During the two meetings, the candidate contradicted himself, telling the parents something they wanted to hear and saying the exact opposite in order to please the teacher group later in the day. His candidacy effectively ended with these interchanges, witnessed by a horrified search-committee member.

Unfortunately, most of us will eventually deal — personally or professionally — with a Head of School who lacks integrity. They say they'll do something, but it never gets done. You have to send them emails to document your conversations because you don't trust they'll remember the conversation or follow up in good faith. Sometimes their responses to feedback or disagreements are defensive, vain, or just plain mean. It's certainly happened to the author of this book, more than once.

I have empathy for Heads of School who seem to lack integrity, as I remember the unreasonable expectations put upon them. Boards expect Heads to be like "G-d on a good day," as the NAIS says, so those who are not comfortable enough to ask for help often end up backed against a wall, defensive, scrambling.

Do everything you can both to have integrity and to build a reputation of integrity. Ask for help when you need it, be honest when you don't know something, and do everything you can to deliver on your promises. The self-management section below will help you deliver on those promises.

S: Self-Management

> *Sometimes they're paying for you to be the grownup in the room.*
>
> —NANCY LEADERMAN,
> *Head of School, The Shalom School, Sacramento, California*

Whether a Head discovers a child-safety issue, bullying, academic dishonesty, a newly discovered financial issue, a conflict among faculty members, or any of a hundred other problems, she is often there to provide calm in the emotional storm. For that reason, a Division Head or staff member prone to emotional outbursts and emotional reactivity is unlikely to be seen as a future leader for their school or any other school. Conversely, a positive, optimistic, orderly, and calm adult is likely to be eyed for a leadership position with great excitement. We will discuss the full extent of self management in this next section: b. Self Management in Detail.

b. The SELF Framework: Self Management

P. L. Travers's fictional wonder-nanny, Mary Poppins, makes a pretty solid model for our discussion about self-management. I use the acronym SELF to refer to the four elements of self-management: Surroundings, Emotions, Look, and Forecasting. Each of these areas matches a Who, What, When, Where, Why, or How Question in one or more ways, as well.

S: Surroundings

> *If your desk (or desktop) is a mess, you might be too. Research shows clutter adds to our stress and anxiety levels, detracts from our ability to focus, and makes us seem less conscientious and agreeable.*
>
> —CLEAN UP YOUR DESK ALREADY,
> *Harvard Business Review, April 2019*

Poppins arrives at the home of the miserable Banks family in 1910 London by *flying* in, using an apparently ordinary umbrella and the supernatural ability to control the wind itself.

In addition to being able to control the wind, Poppins has other relevant superpowers. She can clean a room by snapping her fingers (this is the superpower I would pick), she pulls any obscure item immediately out of her appropriately-sized overnight bag, and she transports people into drawings and back into real life.

There was an internal candidate early in a search we did many years ago who was not seriously considered by his employer as a candidate for a more senior role because he was considered too disorganized. (Of course, he was subsequently hired at an equally excellent school in another state, but that's a topic for another book.)

Ideal Heads of School are organized. They maintain clean, airy, inviting, and uncluttered offices that showcase their diplomas, books, awards, student art, and communities' values. They have solid filing systems, both digital and paper, and they don't misplace important documents. They keep track of facilities-related matters appropriately through delegation and consultation with support staff, as well. They can be trusted to handle matters like accreditation and licensing, both of which require many types of paperwork, filing, and interactions.

E: Emotions

> *[A Head of School is expected to have] controlled passion, steadiness, and [to be] unflappable, reassuring*
>
> — BRENT BETIT,
> *Head of School, The Fletcher School, Charlotte, North Carolina*

Poppins wins the hearts of the Banks children by making even difficult and unpleasant tasks palatable ("In every job that must be done, there is an element of fun.") — in iambic tetrameter, no less! And never forget, "Just a spoonful of sugar helps the medicine go down, in the most delightful way!"

Of all of the aforementioned supernatural abilities, her most incredible skill is the ability to retain her calm and good humor in every situation, no matter how dire.

In real life, our firm conducted a search for a school that excluded a candidate because she was reputed to share frequent, negative feelings with parents at the school. This behavior seems reasonable when you are embedded deeply in your school community, such as when Jewish day-school administrators attend synagogue with Jewish parents in their communities. Unfortunately, complaining to parents or colleagues is behavior that is absolutely inconsistent with the school's marketing and, therefore, with the job description of the Head of School.

The Head of School job is an endless stream of emotional challenges. (For that reason, many people aren't interested in the job!) As is the case for most leaders, everyone will expect you to remain calm, optimistic, and positive at every moment. You have to seek feedback, listen to it without defensiveness (whether you sought it out or not), and respond without anger. You will be expected to have grit and to overcome obstacles in your path. Between your current role and your first Headship (or your next Headship), you will want to develop your reputation for calm positivity. If you need to vent, you need to enlist a romantic partner or a paid therapist, not your colleagues or customers.

Chris Herman sums it up well:

Always responding with positivity and optimism, even when sarcasm would be funny and called for.

—CHRIS HERMAN,
Head of School, The Garden School, Jackson Heights, New York

L: Look

> *[T]here is a common perception among [managers] that if you can't handle the small things, you probably aren't well suited to handle larger responsibility. Put simply: If you can't even dress yourself properly, you can't handle much else.*
>
> —Forbes.com[2]

Despite having just literally flown in, Poppins has nary a hair out of place, and she is dressed perfectly for the occasion, time, and place. The same can be said of her voyages into cartoon-land.

Similarly, as ridiculous as it may sound, Heads of School are expected to *look* the part. What constitutes appropriate dress is regional as well as cultural. Certain cities favor more glamorous appearance, while other regions favor more down-to-Earth attire.

In a religious school, you might be expected to cover certain commonly exposed areas like the hair, shoulders, or knees. Women might be expected to wear skirts or dresses. Men may be expected to wear suits. At the same time, you are expected not to dress *too* religiously, lest you be seen as judging the parent body or affiliated with an "excessively" zealous or fundamentalist branch of your faith tradition.

---

[2]   https://www.forbes.com/sites/quora/2018/11/15/should-people-really-dress-for-the-job-they-want-not-the-job-they-have/?sh=899d70d26364

The upshot? It's fine to ask the recruiter or committee chair what to wear to video and on-site interviews. Most will give you appropriate advice. One easy trick? Look at the attire and appearance of the current administrators on their profile photos on the website. Err on the side of being slightly, but not dramatically, overdressed. Wear nails trimmed and hair neat; you wouldn't believe the sorts of things we've seen over the years.

F: Forecasting

Schools have to think ahead, and the Head has to be the catalyst for [this planning].

— JONATHAN LAMB,
Head of School, Storm King School,
Cornwall-on-Hudson, New York

Poppins can be fun and spontaneous, diving the children into a fictional animated world through a drawing, while she is also prepared and perfectly planned.

Heads of School are expected to have exquisite time-management skills, full stop. You have time to visit classrooms periodically, attend faculty meetings as appropriate, meet with concerned parents as needed, attend or host admissions events and evening board meetings, and more. The time commitment is incredible for Heads, but the demand for time management may be even more intense.

Second in importance to time management is project management. You will be expected to track and follow up with every concern and request in a "spirit of customer service," as many of my client schools say. You respond to emails within 24 hours, follow up from meeting To-Dos, and more. Equally, you have a sense of timing, so you don't email too much or too insistently when an issue remains open on someone else's To-Do list.

Finally, you are proactive. You think ahead, you plan, you prioritize, and you collaborate to ensure that calendars are never in conflict.

If you struggle with time management, seek guidance from a coach or mentor to get on track. Even if your school doesn't have an annual-review system, create goals for yourself to achieve and document your progress with them to teach yourself where you need to put your time each week, month, and year.

c. The Really Hard Parts: Partners and Prejudice

> *Finding good candidates of color, and expanding the diversity and equity of an organization that has been culturally insular and monochromatic... is THE key hiring issue of our times, and the most challenging one in many ways. To publish a book on hiring without addressing this would make the book essentially useless.*
>
> —CEDAR OLIVER,
> *Director of School, Waldorf School of Massachusetts Bay*

Our firm was recently involved in a senior-leadership search with a search-committee member who asked a candidate about her hobbies. The committee collaborated with us to create a carefully choreographed list of behavioral-interview questions based on the priorities they identified at the beginning of the process. This interviewer went off-script and wanted to exclude a candidate from the final round because the candidate "liked to shop" in her free time. This board member was sure that a candidate who liked to shop would be a bad fit for the modest non-profit organization's culture.

When I help train search committees to interview, we use behavioral interviewing ("Please tell us about a time when you" did some part of this job previously) because it is demonstrated to produce better, less-biased hires than freeform interviewing. When we go rogue, so to speak, we tend to focus on how candidates are like us as interviewers, and we hire the people we like or the people who look like us. That's exactly what happened here, and ultimately this school did not hire Ms. Shopper.

Writing this book at the beginning of 2021, JEDI (an acronym for "Justice, Equity, Diversity, and Inclusion") has indeed become a central hiring priority in the public discourse. This priority is even higher in independent schools, which are, as Cedar Oliver put it, "monochromatic." Schools tend to select male leaders at the high-school level, often hiring them over female leaders with a better cultural fit. Independent schools with predominantly white parent bodies tend to hire white senior administrators.

I hardly have flip answers to these painful, centuries-old challenges. In the meantime, I would encourage you to develop the strong "Fit" (as we discussed previously) with each school. If a search committee is earnest in its desire to seek diversity and equity, it will consider your fit in mission, regional culture, school culture, personal connections, and educational philosophy. The search committee will focus less on the color of your skin when making hiring decisions. I hope we are not still having this discussion in ten years, but I fear that we might still be.

How the Process Typically Works

In this chapter, we will walk through how the process typically works so that you can prepare for success and feel confident as you go, regardless of where you are in your career now.

a. Finding Roles

Oftentimes, a recruiter or an outgoing Head of School will contact senior administrators she knows in order to ask them to apply for an open position. For this reason, it's important for you to let your professional network know that you are looking for positions if you can do so without jeopardizing your current position. If your interest has to be confidential, be careful to whom you disclose, but certainly do disclose.

Throughout your career, you'll want to develop and nurture long-term relationships with potential mentors and sponsors (while, in turn, mentoring and sponsoring others). Ask your mentors how they got to their current position and whether they'd help you develop some of the skills they've developed along the way. Stay in touch with them, ask for their advice, and *listen* to their advice. If you can be geographically flexible, pick professional roles based on the partnership you think a Head of School will provide.

Obviously, you'll want to visit job-board websites like HeadofSchoolJobs.com, Educational Directions' Blue Sheet, and NAIS Career Center. Additionally, you should join email lists that contain Headship listings. You can find a full list of places to look at http://TraditionSearchPartners.com/Become.

As soon as possible, develop relationships with search consultants at large and small firms. Let them know when you're considering a search.

Attend regional and national conferences, even online if necessary, become involved in the appropriate leadership groups to increase your visibility within the organization.

At this point, you should create a spreadsheet of positions that interest you. (Include the title, school, location, link, and any other information you feel is relevant to your particular preferences and circumstances.) The next section discusses what to do with that spreadsheet.

b. Applications, Resumes, and Cover Letters

Once you've started looking at a particular school or several, it is essential to devote time to researching the school. It'll set you up to appear "prepared," as discussed previously in the section on F: Fit. More importantly, this research will help you understand the extent to which a school is a potential fit for you and whether to pursue the role.

Take notes about each school. I offer a worksheet on our website so that you can know what information to seek and note. You can find it at http://TraditionSearchPartners.com/Become. Keep a folder (digital or paper) for each school you are interested in so you can keep track of the details.

Read the job description in detail, figure out which CREST and FACTS framework features are most important to a particular school right now and whether those features are a good match for your strengths.

Read the school's website and social media, obviously. Take notes about what you learn, both objectively and subjectively.

If you know anyone in the community that you trust to keep your interest appropriately confidential at this stage, reach out to them.

Google them in case there's some controversy regarding the school, but don't let the controversy stop you from applying. As you did with your own school, you might even register for a Google Alert on each school you are interested in so you can stay up to date on news updates about the school.

Finally, register for a free account with Guidestar.org and look at the school's tax returns (990 forms). These forms will give you a sense of the size of each organization's budget and compensation for its current senior leadership team. Record this information on your spreadsheet and confirm it with the recruiter when you are discussing compensation.

At this level, your cover letter must be custom written for each school, role, and geographical location. We get cover letters every day for Head of School positions that are generic, submitted "To Whom it May Concern," or erroneous in their content. If you are writing a cover letter to submit to a secular Reggio Emilia Inspired preschool program and you write about your commitment to Christian middle-school education, you've ended your candidacy before it even began.

Before you submit your resume, cover letter, and statement of educational philosophy (if required), please have someone review them to ensure they are quality representations of your work.

While you'll want to highlight your achievements in the five CREST framework areas (Communication, Responsibility for people, Enrollment management, Stewardship of finances, and Technical expertise as a master educator), you don't want to include everything you've ever done:

> *Avoid having your resume be more than two pages. Not everything that was relevant the last time you applied is relevant for this job. Highlight the key pieces around experience with things like governance, fundraising, managing and growing faculty and staff, curricular work, etc.*

> —SUMANT BHAT,
> *Head of School, Stanley British Primary School, Denver, Colorado*

c. Screening Interviews

Not all search consultants are all that good, but they are the gauntlet through which all head candidates must pass. If you are a non-traditional candidate, the biases and blindspots of the consultants can weaken your candidacy... I am a non-traditional head because my background is exclusively in admissions, branding, marketing, and financial aid. I am highly entrepreneurial and was always surprised at how hiring committees just couldn't get past that I'm not a former teacher. I've worked in schools for 20 years, so it's not like I don't know what great teaching looks like. Schools don't need me to teach; they need me to lead in exceedingly difficult market conditions.

—AMY JOLLY,
Head of School, Applewild School, Fitchburg, Massachusetts

[I]n the searches where I was ultimately selected as head of school, I felt the support and encouragement of the search consultant. In both cases, they offered helpful advice and coached me how to best "market" my experience and skill set.

—ELIZABETH MORRISON,
Head of School, Antilles School, Antilles, U.S. Virgin Islands

Once you submit your materials, the search consultant and sometimes the search committee chair(s) will review them. If the readers are interested in your resume, they will ask you to speak by phone or video (and potentially with the search-committee chairs). Different search consultants and different schools use different orders and processes here, but a screening interview or two is standard at this point.

The most important question you will be asked, whether for a Head of School job or any other, is why you want the job. The ideal answer is honest and reflects the ways your passion for the school's mission aligns with what you bring: your skills, education, and experience. When this question is answered poorly, it can be hilarious. On one screening interview, a candidate told a search-committee chair that he wanted the job because "his wife said [he] needed to get a full-time job." (Wrong answer!)

It is helpful to know how "behavioral interviews" work as they are the gold standard for interview questions. Behavioral interview questions start with "Tell me about a time when..." and end with a specific question related to the job in which you are interested. For a Head of School, it might be, "Tell me about a time when you were involved in cultivating a major donor" or "...you had to deal with a major scandal in a school setting."

You can answer these questions easily, interestingly, and in a structured manner using the STAR model: Situation, Task, Action, and Result. If the prompt is, "Tell me about a time when you had to counsel a student out of your school," you would set up the Situation about the school, child, and family. You would then explain the Task: what needed to be done. The Action, in this case, would be the various processes you undertook: attempting to help the child succeed at your school, assembling documentation and helping the parents understand how the child is struggling, helping the family find a new placement, and so on. Finally, for the Result, you would talk about what went well and what didn't in this interaction. Ideally, you'd also discuss how the situation informs how you address these issues now.

It's fine, desirable even, to discuss a failure in the short term, but it must reflect well on your ability to learn and grow in the long term. At the same time, there are some stories you should not tell. One Head candidate answered the "Tell me about a time you failed" question by talking about when he left a student *on another continent* by accident. Don't tell that story. Please, please, don't tell that story.

Behavioral-interview questions tend to come in six categories, often referred to using the acronym IMPACT: Individual contribution, Management, Persuasion, Analysis, Challenge/ Creativity, and Teamwork.

Try to have one or two stories handy in each of these areas. Expect to be asked about each CREST-related area, and expect to be asked about your failures. When did you have to persuade someone in a Head-related disagreement, such as a hiring decision? When did you have to find and analyze data about enrollment, marketing, or finances? And so on.

Even if the search committee doesn't pose questions in the behavioral-interview format, offering specific anecdotes is a great way to bridge the tricky, inevitable divide between "The candidate has no vision for our school" and "The candidate has too much vision for our school." If you're asked how you would handle a specific situation, you might say, "I can't answer that question without knowing more about the culture and people involved, but I can tell you my philosophy about these types of matters and give an illustration from my previous experience," and then go on to do both.

You can access our Guide to Behavioral Interviewing at http://TraditionSearchPartners.com/Become if you'd like a more detailed guide to behavioral interviewing.

With solid preparation and knowledge about the school, it should be easy to prepare one to three meaningful questions about the school's current needs. Please do prepare questions that you cannot answer on Google. (Compensation questions can be answered vaguely on the 990s of the school and similar schools.). If you want to ask about compensation, I suggest a gentle question like, "When in the process do you anticipate discussing compensation?" and "Do you have any guidance for me about the compensation range for this position?")

A word about niceties: at this point in the process, you should begin writing thank-you notes. People differ in their approaches to thank-you note formality. In 2021, I think a short but specific email thank-you note is great.

The content of the email is important, though. Think through what you really appreciated and enjoyed about the conversation and reference those things. If possible, provide some value to the recipient of your thank-you notes. You can recommend a book, send a relevant article, or introduce the recipient to someone of value to them.

d. Video Interviews, Hotel Interviews, and Airport Interviews

Create a briefing book on all the aspects of the impending interview—and review, review, review. Finally, be yourself. The prospective head candidate they interview must be the head that shows up. A disconnect here is lethal.

—THOMAS WILSCHUTZ,
Head of School, Solebury School, New Hope, PA

Between the one-on-one screening interviews and the finalist round, you will very likely encounter a search committee interview. In a bygone era, this interview would take place in a hotel conference room near the major airport closest to the school. (Katherine M. Titus, [Head of School, Mercersburg Academy, Mercersburg, Pennsylvania] pointed out that interview processes that never involved a broad campus visit tend to be referred to as "closed" searches). More recently, these interviews tend to occur by video conference, and more searches tend to be "open" and inclusive.

The same rules apply to these next interviews as to the first screening interviews. Prepare by learning about the school and knowing how you would answer IMPACT-category questions that reflect your CREST-framework skills.

Additionally, ask who sits on the search committee. Google them to learn more about their areas of expertise. Look up the board of trustees of the school, and find out about them as well.

We'll discuss more about attire and behavior for these interviews in the section on in-person interviews below.

e. Reference Checking

Following the search-committee interview or interviews, the school will select finalists. Most often, there are two to three finalists, and occasionally there are four. (The case of only one finalist is not an optimal outcome for a school.)

At this stage, the school will likely conduct reference checks using the references you provided. Some schools check references more thoroughly than others: our firm facilitated a search in which the committee co-chair checked twenty-nine references (for one person)!

When I conduct reference checks, I am aware that candidates submit friendly sources who aren't always objective. As a result, I tend to focus on "fit" related questions. "If the school were to hire this person, what type of scaffolding would he need? In which support areas would we want to hire?" I save the "What red flags should we know about?" question for the end of the interview. Be sure you know how your references will answer these questions.

f. In-Person Interviews

When you're a finalist, you're given such insight to the school with board minutes and curriculum maps, PD maps, endowment, and it can feel daunting; the on-campus part was the most important."

—NICOLE DU FAUCHARD,
*Head of School, The Advent School,
Boston, Massachusetts (profiled below)*

[Maybe a parent] had [her] kid suspended and [wants] me to say [in a group interview that] I wouldn't have suspended [her] kid. I have my radar out for that [kind of question]. I assume that, with every question, there is some reason behind why you asked the question. [Some interviewers] have an agenda as well. I didn't want [to be controlled by] their agenda.

—ELIZABETH MORRISON,
Head of School, Antilles School, U.S. Virgin Islands

The Big Reveal: congratulations, you've made it to the in-person finalist round! In the Covid era, people are doing these exhausting cycles of in-person interview rounds online, but everyone is hoping that this era is over before this book is published.

The traditional time to alert your board chair or Head that you're on the job market (if you have not done so already) is when you become a finalist in a search. Ideally, he or she would have been supporting and encouraging you throughout the process, not just at the end, but not everyone has that luxury. Your candidacy will become public information when you step foot on campus, and you want your supervisor to hear this news from you directly.

In-person interviews test your capacities: energy level, positivity, preparation, and listening for fourteen hours a day.

If the school or search consultant has not provided you with materials about the school, including its strategic plan, financial information, enrollment history, and so on, ask for them at this time. Review these materials carefully, adding notes to your portfolio about the school. You may ask for help from a mentor, such as a Head of another school, in reviewing them while maintaining professional confidentiality.

These visits typically last two (long) days or so. You'll meet with trustees, division heads, senior staff members, groups of faculty, groups of parents, sometimes groups of students, sometimes major donors, and community or religious leaders (in the case of a parochial school). If students aren't on the agenda, ask to interact with students, they are the heart of the school.

If you have a spouse or partner, he will probably be invited on the trip since partners participate in decision making for the family. The search committee will invite him to visit the school, tour the area, view houses in the area with a realtor (if the job does not provide a house), and meet peers socially. Please be warned that the school is assessing your spouse as they wine and dine him.

A funny word of advice from nearly every Head I interviewed: bring pocket snacks and water bottles. Accept any bathroom break, even if it's just for a minute to breathe and relax. Eat and drink as frequently as possible — between meetings — to maintain your energy level.

Another funny word of advice from a few Heads: be prepared to be left in a room with a group of people and no agenda. You may have to "drive" the conversation by asking questions about them or even telling funny stories. Appropriate humor goes a long way. Keep the tone as positive as possible.

Between meetings, after your bathroom break, take notes so that your follow-up can be detailed and efficient. (It's okay to say you don't know the answer to a question. Plan to follow up with an answer in these cases.)

Toward the end of the interview cycle, you will likely meet with the full board and search committee. The magic words to share at the end of this process: "If offered the job, I would accept it." Knowing that you are interested will help a school commit to you in much the same way that my twelfth-grade English teacher told me that men don't propose marriage unless they're sure they'd get a "yes" in reply.

Finally, know that you will make it to the finalist round two or three times before making a match. If you are not selected, ask for feedback from the search consultant or school, if possible. Ask for advice from your mentors through the process and afterward, and make an effort to strengthen your CREST, FACTS, and SELF skills as needed.

g. Contract Negotiation

Believe in your worth and do your homework.

—BRENT BETIT,
Head of School, The Fletcher School, Charlotte, North Carolina

The most important advice I can give you in this section is this: you will *need* an employment lawyer because of the many complex and restrictive clauses in a Head contract. Ask Head friends which attorney they used and what tips they have about the process. Use someone who specifically has experience negotiating Head contracts since they're unique.

If you struggle to negotiate on your own behalf, ask a partner or friend to help you behind the scenes. Negotiation research suggests that it's okay to "go high" in requests once you're a finalist for the position, but make sure to maintain a committed, enthusiastic, and positive attitude throughout the process.

Come armed with research via 990s and competitive market analysis. Look at NAIS compensation surveys nationally and regionally. Know that compensation varies by region but has to be competitive enough to attract candidates who could move anywhere. Lower schools tend to pay less than middle schools, which pay less than upper schools, which pay less than fully integrated K-12 schools. Larger schools pay more than smaller schools, in general.

Use integrative bargaining. Don't get stuck only on a single salary line. Ask about tuition discounts for children or grandchildren. Ask about housing: sometimes there is a Head's house, and other times there is a budget for assistance for purchasing a house. Ask about a budget for professional development, such as conference attendance. There might also be a budget for a Head of School coach, which you want if you're a first-time Head. You may want the right to continue doing consulting work or remain on the adjunct faculty at a local university.

I offer a template for contract terms with more detail at http://TraditionSearchPartners.com/Become in case you're interested in seeing samples.

h. Announcement and Transition

Congratulations on your success! Now that you're in a school-transition process, treading carefully can have a huge, positive impact on your future.

First and foremost, be good to the school you're departing. You should have advised your current board chair or Head earlier in the process that you were involved in the search process. At this point, you will let him or her know first, in person or by phone, that you have been offered and accepted a position.

You will work with the new school and the old school to time public announcements thoughtfully. Make sure your current colleagues and parents find out directly, not from scuttlebutt from your new community. Keep your mentor/mentee relationships as strong as possible as you transition to your new school.

Work with your new board president and senior leadership to drive the transition process to your new school. Make sure the board has assembled a transition committee, and plan to make up to three trips to the new school during the second semester of the school year if possible.

If this book helped you achieve your goal, would you please email me to let me know? My email is lydia@TraditionSearchPartners.com, and I read and reply to all emails myself.

CHAPTER FOUR

Case Studies: Paths to Headship

I took an unorthodox path. I served in the military for four years and then went into finance and banking before taking my first position as a CFO at an independent school. I made it a point to learn all I could about independent schools, I taught classes and coached the baseball team. I fully immersed myself in school life. I also relied heavily on mentors who helped me and still do.

—STUART HIRSTEIN,
Head of School, Saint Edward's School, Vero Beach, Florida

Real-life case studies help provide color to a potentially black-and-white depiction of this process; so let's look at a few Heads who agreed to be profiled. Each case study highlights a different path to Headship. I hope you will see aspects of your situation in some of them — and that you find the similarities instructive.

There are other paths, too, so do feel creative license to navigate your own way through. Once you have one Headship on your resume, you will rarely be asked again about what came prior.

a. The Traditional Path: Jon Kidder, Barrie Academy

While the "typical" path is from Division Head to Head, this may not be the best model. Division Heads and other Department Leaders are often mired in daily management functions and may not have the experience to see the entire organization in order to plan for its successful growth and development over time.

— DAVID MAHLER,
Head of School, The Out-of-Door Academy, Sarasota, Florida

The "standard" path to independent-school Headship might be: you finish your own education with a bachelor's or master's degree, and you start as a teacher at an independent school. You become a lead teacher a few years later. Eventually, you become a principal of an elementary, middle, or high school. At a large school, you might become a "division head," overseeing the education and operations of an elementary, middle, or high school. You do all of this growth within a single school or moving every five years or so to obtain a promotion. If you move — but not too often — you advance faster.

At this point, you may enroll in a doctorate in educational administration or one of the Aspiring Heads programs.

You will probably switch schools in order to become a Head. If you move to a large school, an intermediate step may be a lateral move to become principal of a larger student body or Assistant Head of School. Two moves down the road, you would be a good candidate for Head of School. If you land immediately at a small school, you may go directly from principal to Head of School.

> *[To rise up from teaching to principal to Division Head to Head of School,] you need experience you can't get, like Screen Actors Guild jobs or budgeting experience.*
>
> —Anonymous Head of School

The tricky thing about this path, as our quoted Heads alluded to above, is that nothing about being a teacher, principal, or division head really helps you develop most of the skills required to be a Head of School. In most schools, the principal handles the educational and some personnel decisions while the Head handles the other CREST-framework tasks of running a school: fundraising, managing the board, managing the finances, and so on.

As you can probably tell by now, if you want to take this traditional path, you are going to need to develop skills proactively and outside of the job description of a teacher, principal, or division head who does not handle most of the CREST responsibilities. Jon Kidder, Head at Barrie School in Silver Spring, Maryland, provides an illustrative case study about how to navigate this path — especially in terms of the critical role that mentors can play in supporting an educator's journey on the path toward leadership.

Jon was a junior in high school himself when a move from public school to a selective-enrollment Polytechnic School in Pasadena, California opened his eyes to "what a school could be… and this experience profoundly changed [his] life." He had always wanted to be a teacher, he said, because he saw that teachers "consistently found joy and purpose in their work." In the independent-school setting, he saw unique opportunities to fulfill that promise fully.

He became a teaching assistant during high school and college. During college, Jon helped found a program to support first-generation college-bound high school students from public schools in Pasadena. Once he graduated, he became a public-school teacher for one year after college but quickly got a job at Polytechnic, becoming a teacher and half-time administrator there. During this early part of his career, he taught history and mathematics, and also explored administrative responsibilities by running the summer high school program for public school students, organizing school's outdoor education programs, and a leading a writer's center.

Interested in administration in independent schools, Jon enrolled in an evenings-and-weekends doctoral program in education at UCLA "at the suggestion of Debbie Reed, his Head of School at the time at the Polytechnic School." He met his wife there, as well. His dissertation compared independent, charter, and public-school board governance.

Doctorate in hand, his Head Debbie Reed then suggested he interview for his first Assistant Headship, running a middle and high school at the Pilgrim School in Los Angeles under Dr. Mark Brooks. "He was the toughest person I ever worked for and I am so grateful for all he taught me about leadership, the importance of having a relentless work ethic, and how to steward a community."

Following four years in that role at Pilgrim, Jon then took a second Assistant Headship running the high school at The Drew School in San Francisco under Sam Cuddeback.

Just over two years into that role, his Head of School suggested he apply to the Park Day School to take over for Tom Little, a Head of School who was unfortunately diagnosed with terminal cancer after a successful twenty-five year tenure there. Cuddeback and Little were close friends and influential educational leaders in the region. Cuddeback felt Jon could serve as an Interim Head and then short-term permanent Head to steward the school through its period of mourning.

His Headship at the ninety-year-old Barrie School in Silver Spring, Maryland came four years later. Debbie Reed at Polytechnic referred him to Barrie through her relationship with the recruiter conducting the national search.

Jon said that he had been "offered a couple of Headships at other places" but turned them down because Barrie School was always his first choice. They are "inclusive" in their admissions, with diversity in "race, ethnicity, and social class." He loved the ability to work on a large "canvas" of the pre-K through twelfth grade programs. He wanted a progressive school with an engaging, student-centered pedagogical framework and he loved that Barrie School's "classrooms look and feel like the United Nations" where "the children are truly representative of the world's diversity and no student is made to feel like 'the different one.'"

Through each of these roles, he says he hopes to "create for others the learning environments he wishes he had had" in primary and secondary schools, feeling that "the independent-school model was the best way to do that."

When he was in college "dreaming about" these leadership roles, he thought he would spend his time thinking about curriculum. In reality, Heads are "like mayors of small communities," and most of their time is spent "solving really challenging problems" to steward the financial and emotional wellness of the community. "The nature of this role is that Heads of School mostly get intractable, complex problems that usually need a truly collaborative approach to solve," he said. "The reality," Jon shared, "is that the day-to-day role is not particularly glamorous, but it is crucial for supporting a healthy school community and culture and you have to truly love the work."

One of the challenges that Jon shared is that Heads of School rarely get the formal training necessary to prepare to tackle the wide range of challenges they encounter: from budgeting to admissions to marketing to facilities management to human resources to fundraising to ways to run a successful capital campaign. He says, "The only way to prepare for this wide-range of challenges is to seek out and cultivate mentorships from current Heads of School, to stay in touch with them, to build a network of other leaders we can engage with, and to take on leadership positions early in our careers where we can learn from experienced and engaging mentors."

"Getting mentorship from a Head of School is one of the most crucial things you can do,"Jon recommends, developing relationships with seasoned leaders who teach you about both the role and help you along the path to obtaining it. Jon felt he "hit the gold mine" in mentorship from Debbie Reed, Mark Brooks, and Sam Cuddeback throughout the course of his career. "While amazing mentors may come your way, it is on us as aspiring leaders to cultivate these relationships as well as deliberately seek out individuals who want to 'pay it forward' and mentor the next generation of leaders."

b. The Internal Candidate: Drew Casertano and Jon Downs, Millbrook School

> *Succession Planning on both the Board and Head of School level should be a regular discussion topic at each meeting of both groups. This discipline normalizes identifying those within the school who should be invested in to remotely prepare persons for leadership positions.*
>
> —DONALD F. REILLY,
> *Head of School, Malvern Preparatory School, Malvern, Pennsylvania*

Drew Casertano of Millbrook School has spent the last five years (as of this writing) building capacity in his planned successor at Millbrook, Assistant Headmaster Jon Downs. Drew has brought Jon into every aspect of Headship, at the request of its board of trustees, sharing with Jon everything Drew has learned in his thirty-one years in that seat.

So, I was not surprised when another interviewee, Liz Morrison of Antilles School, told me she had also previously worked for one Drew Casertano. Drew had helped her prepare for and obtain *her* first Headship. He obviously takes his role seriously in developing new Heads and investing in the careers of those who work with him. Drew is a rare example of a leader in this regard, and a tremendously successful one at that.

Looking back, Drew was already in his eighth year as Head when a senior named Jon Dows graduated from Millbrook. After graduating in 1998, Jon went on to get his bachelor's degree and two master's degrees in English and education, focusing on independent-school leadership, very much intending to work toward a Headship.

During and after his master's studies, Jon served Newark Academy in Livingston, New Jersey as a teacher, coach, and junior admissions representative, actively building his CREST skills.

In 2008, Jon went on to Providence Day School to take on the role of dean of students.

It was 2010 when Jon returned to Millbrook as the Admissions Director. The school's website announced him as having been "Student Council president, an all-school prefect, a 12-letter athlete and three-sport captain, and winner of both the Sportsmanship Cup and the Class of 1978 Award" during his time as a boarding student at Millbrook. And Jon really is the living, breathing embodiment of Millbrook.

In 2015, the board asked Jon to commit himself to five years learning the Head of School role from Drew. Jon agreed. In the best case, Jon would take over from Drew upon his departure from Millbrook after over thirty years. In the worst case, Jon would have served a five-year apprenticeship that positioned him well to take over the Headship of nearly any independent school.

Jon and Drew both recommend that aspiring Heads reading this book to tell your Head of your interest in learning from him or her about the Head role rather than waiting to be plucked from obscurity at random in some Platonic ideal of how leadership works. If your Head helps to groom you for the role, you are many steps closer to achieving it. If your Head isn't interested in helping you and you are still committed to your goal, you will likely need a new position or a new Head.

In addition to their solid advice, I'd like to add: be aware that internal candidates are seen as risky and potentially disruptive, as this anonymous Head commented:

"Internal candidates were disruptive to the community and the search process."

In light of this risk and disruption, I would like to give you two pieces of advice if you're pursuing internal candidacy over the objections of so many—

First, when discussions about a transition start, talk with your current Head and board president, if appropriate and separately at first, about whether each supports your candidacy. Even with a supported and qualified internal candidate like Jon Downs, the school will very likely want to conduct a national search. Without support, the school will not hire you. You should pursue actionable feedback about why they don't support your candidacy and act on that feedback.

Second, if you have their support, be upfront that you will do everything you can to act discreetly and professionally throughout the process. I have seen internal candidates cause disruption by stoking the passions of fan clubs of parents and teachers who support their candidacies. This approach is not effective, and it taints you as unprofessionally placing yourself above the needs of the school. Being the adult in the room is one of the job qualifications. Demonstrate your ability to do so starting now, if you haven't already.

It doesn't hurt if you're an alumnus of the school and a living embodiment of its mission, vision, and values, either.

c. From Staff to Head, From Higher Ed to Head: Nicole A. DuFauchard, The Advent School

Our next case study represents two different paths to Headship: starting as staff rather than faculty and starting in higher education rather than primary or secondary education.

As Headship has become more about the CREST skillset of business management and leadership and less about curriculum and instruction, boards have opened their minds to candidates with non-traditional backgrounds. Another benefit of this broadened mindset is that it opens schools to a more diverse candidate pool. While the "traditional" candidate pool is usually filled with those educated by independent schools, white people, men, and those benefiting from intergenerational wealth, the "non-traditional" candidate pool is statistically more diverse ethnically, intellectually, and philosophically.

Nicole A. du Fauchard, Head of the Advent School of Boston, Massachusetts, is a perfect example of a staff member who became a Head through this non-traditional path that is growing in popularity. Additionally, she came from the world of higher education, which is also a non-traditional path many try to navigate as they grow weary of higher education. You can see her collect the CREST skills on her resume almost systematically in preparation for Headship.

Nicole began with three positions in higher education, building experience in communication and leadership. First, she served as the Resident Director at SUNY Morrisville. For her second position, she spent time at Trinity Washington University as the Director of Campus Activities — Multicultural Affairs. Her third role was as Director of Alumni Affairs at Hunter College in New York.

When Nicole moved to Hands on Charlotte as its External Affairs Director, she began to build her portfolio in the nonprofit-leadership space outside of higher education. As the Director of Development of the Charlotte Ballet, she transitioned more directly into the fundraising and financial stewardship role that she would later need as a Head.

Nicole obtained her first role in the independent-school world in 2006 as the Director of Multicultural Affairs at Providence Day School. During her seven years in this role, she served on the Girl Talk Foundation board, gaining experience in the board-relations part of the CREST skillset.

In 2013, she was finally ready to leave Providence for her own Headship at The Advent School in Boston. In addition to her service as a Head, Nicole continues to broaden her CREST skillset. She teaches programs at the National Association of Independent Schools, is a part-time faculty member at the Longy School of Music, and serves on two nonprofit boards.

Nicole had two pieces of advice for non-traditional candidates seeking Headship in the primary or secondary space:

First, when asked about your CREST skills, point the interviewers to your experiences even if they aren't as direct as if you had traversed the traditional path. For example, if you served on the board of a nonprofit, you have board-relations experience. If you served as the treasurer of a school's board, you have relevant budgeting experience. We'll see similar advice from Susan Paynter in e. From Public to Independent, From Trustee to Head: Susan Paynter, High Meadow School.

Second, seek out classroom teaching experience at some level and teach a class while you're on campus as a first-time administrator, staff member, or Head. Classroom experience provides you with the educational credibility schools seek, and simply taking the initiative will go a long way. Coming from the higher education world also helps because you give credence to the idea that you understand one of the important end goals of independent-school education.

We see in Nicole's profile an example of how you can use your staff experiences and volunteer-leadership roles to build toward your first Headship. Next, we will look at Interim Headship, a challenging path in itself.

d. The Interim Headship: Johnny Graham, Williamsburg Christian Academy

Several of the people mentioned in this book served as Interim Head or Acting Head at some point in their careers. Sometimes, this role will lead to your hiring as a permanent Head of School. Other times, it will prepare you for a permanent Headship elsewhere. In a third case, Interim Headship might be a role you wish to take on serially; some people enjoy the transitional years in an organization. Finally, you may learn through Interim Headship that Headship just isn't for you. (It's not a job for everyone!)

Until Future-Dr. Johnny Graham found a spiritual and organizational home at Williamsburg Christian Academy in 2019, he served several schools at transitional points.

Himself a "boarding school product," he knew that boarding school was a "lifestyle he enjoyed and loved." Like so many Heads of School, Johnny started his career as both a history teacher and an athletic coach. (This pattern is so common that I almost want to tell aspiring Heads that they should all coach athletic teams.)

Johnny would serve four more schools as a teacher, coach, and administrator before serving in a senior-leadership role. He served the McCallie School as an advanced history teacher and house parent for two dorms. In his next role, he taught history and coached basketball at The Westminster Schools. After that, he built more of the CREST skills at the Howard School as its Athletic Director, Summer-Programs Director, After-School Director, *and* Head Boys Varsity Basketball Coach!

At the boarding and day school Brandon Hall School in Atlanta, Johnny served his first Assistant Headship, managing many of the same areas he managed at Howard. It was there that he would serve a year as Interim Head in an urgent situation, "as fate would have it."

After his interim term, Johnny took a job with a "Chinese investment company" looking to open a boarding school for international students, many of whom came from China. "They were pretty clear from the jump, they wanted it to be for Chinese students and have Chinese leadership." So he founded and built the school but never thought he would be the long-term Head there due to that cultural misalignment. Once he finished his work as a founder, he was ready to find a permanent role.

Most Heads will tell you that it's much easier to find second and subsequent Headships since most schools seek experienced Heads. Given his choice of Headships, Johnny chose the one that fit with his spiritual and organizational background: Williamsburg Christian Academy, a boarding school in line with his experience in boarding schools.

Having been promoted internally to Interim Head, Johnny credits his "elite" training at "first-rate" boarding and day schools and his "persona that fit as a no-nonsense, by-the-book tone setter where discipline and those things could be addressed so the Head could fundraise and do Head things and not have to worry about any internal operations of the school" as optimal for that selection process.

As with many Interim Heads, the Interim role gave Johnny "an amazing skill set that now [has served me well] as a three-time Head of School and former Founding Head. Those skills [include] dealing with legal challenges, [handling] internal crises, [developing] the faculty, [and addressing] enrollment issues. As an Interim, you plug your finger in the dike for 16 to 18 months [to prepare for] a permanent Head of School. You deal with major legal challenges, major recruitment challenges, major personnel issues, major messaging issues."

If you enjoy the crisis-management aspect of school leadership, serial Interim Headship may appeal to you. And if you are looking for a drinking-from-the-firehose approach to putting a Headship on your resume as soon as possible, finding an Interim role can help you do so, as well.

e. From Public to Independent, From Trustee to Head: Susan Paynter, High Meadow School

Our next case study also represents two increasingly common paths to Headship: from public-school administration to independent Headship and from a community member (e.g., trustee and grandparent) to Head of School.

> *[Being a] public-school assistant superintendent with 10,000 children and 500 teachers was much easier than [being] a charter leader or private school Head of School. In a Headship, you don't have [the same level] of admin support.*
>
> —SUSAN PAYNTER,
> *Head of School, High Meadow School, Stone Ridge, New York*

After a long and successful career in public education, High Meadow School grandmother Susan Paynter offered to provide a free professional-development session in differentiation in mathematics instruction to the faculty at her grandchildren's "academically rigorous, highly outdoor, child-centered" school.

After that hour, Susan says that the school asked her to work as an educational consultant. She happily consulted for a period of years, teaching faculty new techniques for differentiation in mathematics instruction and for writing curriculum to support this differentiation in action.

After some time, High Meadow asked Susan to serve on the school board as its "education chair." (That position is no longer common on independent-school boards because it crosses the barrier of governance into the school's operations.) When High Meadow eventually needed an Interim Head of School, Susan was already embedded in the community and available to serve. Finally, she transitioned to become High Meadow's permanent Head of School following confirmation of the hire through a national search for other candidates.

I advise people interested in teaching in independent schools to join the substitute-teacher list for these schools in advance for much the same reason: be a known commodity as a professional for when a position opens. Just being a community member isn't enough since, as we've seen, there are risks in hiring community members.

A word of warning: it is very unusual for a trustee to transition successfully to a Headship, even though many trustees think it's a job they could do successfully. Few have the CREST skills, the FACT skills, and the SELF characteristics to learn what to do and do it well. If you are a trustee reading this book in order to fashion yourself as a Head, I encourage you to proceed with caution.

Back to High Meadow, Susan has been the Head of School for several years as of this writing. She has a lot of insight to offer about the transition from public to independent-school administration. She says there is a real disconnect between the two; it is easier to lead a public school system with 10,000 children and 500 teachers than lead an independent school with 170 students.

"Be true to your heart and your principles," Susan says, as the Head of an independent school. In a public-school system, you are "showing data sets and an academic background." In an independent school, "You have to get in touch with what your heart is telling you matters for kids."

"Public schools lose out by going with the 'flavor of the month'" in terms of academic trends, Susan says. In an independent school, there is — and should be — a greater balance between maintaining tradition and instituting new programs.

Susan's technical skills in budgeting came in handy during routine financial challenges at her school (as happens at most schools). Previously, at a charter school, Susan built zero-based budgets and was, therefore, well-positioned to tackle the problem again.

"The biggest difference between public and [independent schools] is fundraising. You don't need to fundraise in public [schools]. In charter, you have to deal with admissions because you're doing recruiting. So I was prepared for everything except development. I had to do a lot of reading and prepare for that area." Susan advises that you "get some side experience. Are you going to be comfortable asking donors for money, making those relationships? However you can get yourself trained, working with a not-for-profit, working as a volunteer, anything to get some background in that area."

During the interview process, Susan advises keeping a particular child in mind. And, "During your leadership, if you can keep the child at the center, there is no decision where that isn't the most relevant."

Additionally, "you need to help interviewers understand what is the same about charter and [independent] or public and [independent]" schools... You have to help them understand. You have to know the new school well enough to constantly make that connection, so they know how well prepared you are."

Part of understanding how to communicate is understanding that "the role of the board in public and [independent] schools is very, very different. In public, [for example,] you have to get [their] approval for textbooks and hiring." In an independent school, the Head and faculty make these decisions while the board supports the Head.

As you navigate from community member to Head or from public-school administration to Headship, Susan's example of balancing tradition with innovation, of bringing experience tempered by a growth mindset, and of bridging gaps through consciousness about similarities and differences between worlds is an excellent one to follow.

f. Build Your Own School: Gabriela Tejedor

Last but not least: in the realm of "non-traditional" paths to Headship, building your own school is an almost unheard-of path, but it's one Gabriela Tejedor and Kelsey Jones took when founding Brooklyn Independent Middle School.

Gabriela and Kelsey taught together at a network charter school in Brooklyn before becoming founding co-Heads of School. In their spare time as teachers, they also tutored students at well-resourced public schools. They saw — and were discouraged by — the differences in attitude between their school and the well-resourced public schools their tutoring clients attended. Here's what Gabriela wrote in an article for the74million.org:

"The students I tutored shared stories about their robotics and coding classes, their theater and visual arts electives, ideas for their STEM projects — and in these exchanges, I started to realize these experiences weren't just about acquiring skills. What was actually being transferred to the students I tutored was the audacity to dream, to explore and to build passions.

At my charter school, students were expected to perform well on a standardized state test. For the students I tutored, it was about developing their voices, having bold ideas and learning about the world around them. The contrast became very clear to me: There are schools for students who we think need structure and others for students who we think deserve creativity. And what this then translated to me was that when our students are segregated, we create different expectations. Different realities. We assume and dream and wish and push differently."

Deciding they wanted to start a charter school with the attitude of a well-resourced public school, Gabriela and Kelsey went immediately from being teachers to being Heads. They relied on an entrepreneurial approach to building a school to attempt to resolve these inequities.

At first, they had to ask lots of questions, like, "What is a business plan?" They sought out mentors who could explain to them what was wrong with the budgets they had outlined. Through their professional networks, they met with Heads of other schools to ask questions about how they started and operated their schools. There was a lot of "lingo" to learn in each of the CREST-framework areas.

Selling themselves as expert educators on a mission — and, now, with a draft business plan — Gabriela and Kelsey sought to build a board of directors. They connected with as many people as possible, asking for introduction after introduction. They eventually persuaded an experienced independent-school trustee to join them as their board chair. The added credibility of an experienced board chair "changed everything" for the pair, legitimizing their vision in the eyes of other potential board members and donors.

They began to recruit parents and children by canvassing local elementary schools for parents who were interested in "a sliding-scale private middle school with a focus on racial and socio-economic diversity" offering a full day of "field learning" on Fridays, "maker learning," and Latin study.

Gabriela credits her and Kelsey's "really strong follow-up" for their success in recruiting students and families. They offered free events like coding and tennis camps, taking notes about and photos of each child, talking with parents about their visions. Using their spreadsheets of information about each student and family, being a prospective BKI family became a very "individualized" experience.

Additionally, their strength in transparent communication helped them recruit and retain families. Parents knew they had no school building at the outset, and they didn't pretend to have resources they didn't have. They were "persistent and transparent" in "constant communication" that "everyone can appreciate."

As of this writing, the school is open and thriving. Gabriela and Kelsey's philosophy and the school's operations attract new students and teachers. Should you wish to open your own unique school, their learning process is an outstanding template.

If none of the paths above is yours exactly, don't let your innovation deter you. Just plow your own path, and don't forget to send me your story so I can include it in the second edition of this book!

CHAPTER FIVE

Conclusion: Where To Go From Here

Whether you are in the midst of searching for a Head position or starting out building your skill sets, you are now armed with the wisdom of scores of Heads to prepare to execute your own search effectively. Use the CREST framework when you think about areas where your resume needs development. Review the FACTS framework to think about how you interact with others before, during, and after your search process. Finally, review the SELF framework periodically to think about how you manage yourself as an individual and as a leader.

And please do visit http://TraditionSearchPartners.com/Become to utilize our workbook and other resources to help you achieve success in the process.

Finally, I wanted to leave the last words to the Heads of School who contributed to this book. They deserve deference for their generosity and wisdom.

First, prepare for a shift in perspective:

Prepare a mentality shift [as you rise into your first Headship]. Division heads are often on their own solving problems and report when they're solved. That's not the relationship heads and board chairs have. [Ask yourself] What have I not shared with my board chair today? ... Never worry alone.

—CHRIS HERMAN,
Head of School, The Garden School, Jackson Heights, New York

Remember that these search processes are taxing on aspiring Heads:

Head searches can be grueling and riddled with so many ups and downs and ebbs and flows. Most heads who enter a search are not properly prepared for these more emotional challenges.

—DEAN J. FUSTO,
President and Head of School, Brandon Hall School, Atlanta, Georgia

Assess the school even as the school assesses you:

Don't forget you get to assess them and you should assess them as much as they're assessing you.

—ELIZABETH MORRISON,
Head of School, Antilles School, Antilles, U.S. Virgin Islands

Finally, be attuned to what excites you, as it may signal a potential fit for you:

If your mind is racing about the work you can do there, this might be the job for you.

—Nicole du Fauchard,
Head of School, The Advent School, Boston, Massachusetts

Congratulations and best wishes as you proceed through your search.

ACKNOWLEDGMENTS

I was amazed and overwhelmed by the breadth and diversity of interest in this book. Scores of Heads shared their personal experiences with me. The Heads I quoted are all named in this book except for several who wanted to remain anonymous. My contributors' generosity is matched only by the insight and depth of their responses.

This book would not be possible without the copy editors, beta readers, and friends who contributed to its shaping. Covie Edwards-Pitt, an old friend and author-mentor, helped me to understand and succeed at the process of writing books.

The wonderful Mireille Chait helped me build Tradition Search Partners; Dr. Dan Ahlstrom was my one-time co-founder of the firm; and Skip Kotkins of Carney Sandoe remains a supportive mentor. Our firm is also a proud supporter of the National Association of Independent Schools (NAIS).

I am eternally indebted to my parents and grandparents, who sacrificed so much as new immigrants to the United States to provide my sister and me with the best education available, as well as to the educators and child-care providers who implemented that education and upbringing. My sister, Mara, reads and listens to endless drafts and ideas, and she even proofreads contracts for me.

Benjamin: you have made my life so utterly different than it would otherwise have been. Thank you for everything you do.

Talia, Avi, Noah, and Eli: Watching you love one another is easily the most profound joy I have ever known. I dedicate this book — and everything else — to you. Take care of each other always.

In addition to the workbook and other resources at http:// TraditionSearchPartners.com/Become, I recommend reviewing the following books as you prepare for your search and your next Headship.

- To do well in interviews, I recommend reading *60 Seconds and You're Hired!: Revised Edition* by Robin Ryan. Like this book, it's a quick and practical read with lots of examples.

- For more on strengthening your interpersonal skills as a leader, check out the excellent *What Got You Here Won't Get You There: How Successful People Become Even More Successful* by Marshall Goldsmith.

- When you interview on campus, and when you start your new Headship, you can use the Baldrige Performance Excellence Framework, produced by the National Institute of Standards and Technology (NIST), to identify the current areas of strength and weakness in operations at a school.

- There are several Aspiring Head of School or New Head of School programs you may consider if you prefer a longer program of study. You can find a list of these programs on our website at http://TraditionSearchPartners.com/Become.

- As you prepare to take the helm of a new school, check out *The First 90 Days, Updated and Expanded: Proven Strategies for Getting Up to Speed Faster and Smarter* by Michael Dawkins. It's really for first-time managers, which you probably aren't, but it can help you sharpen your startup toolkit.

Thank you for reading! Best wishes, and do keep in touch.

Author Lydia Musher is the founder of Tradition Search Partners, a former business-school professor, an experienced school and nonprofit board member, and the mother of independent-school students. Typically called in as "fixers" for tough education-leadership searches, Tradition utilizes aggressive and tested processes, advanced technology and data, and white-glove service that trustees expect in for-profit work.

Lydia is an entrepreneur, writer, and speaker who holds an MBA in marketing and entrepreneurial management from The Wharton School of the University of Pennsylvania as well as MEng and ScB degrees in computer science from the Massachusetts Institute of Technology. She uses her experience and education in leadership and technology to increase professional success and connection in the workplace. Learn more about her at lydiamusher.com.

www.ingramcontent.com/pod-product-compliance
Lightning Source LLC
Chambersburg PA
CBHW051432090426
42737CB00014B/2936